The Philosophy of Bergson

THE

PHILOSOPHY OF BERGSON

BY THE

Hon. Bertrand Russell

LECTURER AND LATE FELLOW OF TRINITY COLLEGE, CAMBRIDGE

WITH A REPLY

BY

Mr. H. WILDON CARR

SECRETARY OF THE ARISTOTELIAN SOCIETY

AND A REJOINDER BY MR. RUSSELL

Published for "The Heretics" by

BOWES AND BOWES

Cambridge

London: Macmillan and Co, Ltd.
Glasgow: Jas. MacLehose and Sons

1914

Mr. Russell's criticism of M. Bergson was read before " The Heretics," in Trinity College, on March 11th, 1913, and was afterwards published in *The Monist*, July, 1912.

Mr. Carr's reply, and Mr. Russell's rejoinder, appeared in *The Cambridge Magazine* for April 12th and April 26th, 1913, respectively.

The Society is indebted to the editors of both papers for permission to republish.

With regard to the value of the following pages as an authoritative account of two of the leading tendencies in modern philosophic thought, it is perhaps worth while to record that M. Bergson wrote to the Editor of *The Cambridge Magazine*, in reply to a request that he should contribute to the discussion himself —

" Je trouve excellente la réponse que Mr. Wildon Carr a déjà faite, et qui porte sur les points spéciaux visés par la critique de Mr. Russell."

THE PHILOSOPHY
OF BERGSON.*

The classification of philosophies is effected, as a rule, either by their methods or by their results : "empirical" and "*a priori*" is a classification by methods, "realist" and "idealist" is a classification by results. An attempt to classify Bergson's philosophy in either of these ways is hardly likely to be successful, since it cuts across all the recognised divisions.

But there is another way of classifying philosophies, less precise, but perhaps more helpful to the non-philosophical, in this way, the principle of division is according to the predominant desire which has led the philosopher to philosophize   Thus we shall have philosophies of feeling inspired by the love of happiness, theoretical philosophies, inspired by the love of knowledge, and practical philosophies, inspired by the love of action.

Among philosophies of feeling we shall place all those which are primarily optimistic or pessimistic, all those that offer schemes of salvation or try to prove that salvation is impossible, to this class belong most religious philosophies. Among theoretical philosophies we shall place most of the

---

* The abbreviations of the titles of the works of M Bergson referred to are . C. E . *Creative Evolution* , M. and M , *Matter and Memory* ; *T and F. W* , *Time and Free Will*   The references are to the English translations of M. Bergson's books.

great systems ; for though the desire for knowledge is rare,
it has been the source of most of what is best in philosophy.
Practical philosophies, on the other hand, will be those which
regard action as the supreme good, considering happiness
an effect and knowledge a mere instrument of successful
activity. Philosophies of this type would have been common
among Western Europeans if philosophers had been average
men , as it is, they have been rare until recent times, in fact
their chief representatives are the pragmatists and M. Bergson.
In the rise of this type of philosophy we may see, as M. Bergson
himself does, the revolt of the modern man of action against
the authority of Greece, and more particularly of Plato ; or
we may connect it, as Dr. Schiller apparently would, with
imperialism and the motor car The modern world calls
for such a philosophy, and the success which it has achieved
is therefore not surprising.

M. Bergson's philosophy, unlike most of the systems of
the past, is dualistic the world, for him, is divided into two
disparate portions, on the one hand life, on the other matter,
or rather that inert something which the intellect views as
matter. The whole universe is the clash and conflict of two
opposite motions life, which climbs upward, and matter,
which falls downward Life is one great force, one vast
vital impulse, given once for all from the beginning of the
world, meeting the resistance of matter, struggling to break
a way through matter, learning gradually to use matter by
means of organisation , divided by the obstacles it encounters
into diverging currents, like the wind at the street corner ;
partly subdued by matter through the very adaptations
which matter forces upon it ; yet retaining always its capacity
for free activity, struggling always to find new outlets, seeking
always for greater liberty of movement amid the opposing
walls of, matter.

Evolution is not primarily explicable by adaptation to
environment ; adaptation explains only the turns and twists
of evolution, like the windings of a road approaching a town
through hilly country. But this simile is not quite adequate ;

there is no town, no definite goal. at the end of the road along which evolution travels. Mechanism and teleology suffer from the same defect . both suppose that there is no essential novelty in the world. Mechanism regards the future as implicit in the past, since it believes the future to be calculable ; teleology also, since it believes that the end to be achieved can be known in advance, denies that any essential novelty is contained in the result.

As against both these views, though with more sympathy for teleology than for mechanism, M. Bergson maintains that evolution is truly *creative*, like the work of an artist. An impulse to action, an undefined want, exists beforehand, but until the want is satisfied it is impossible to know the nature of what will satisfy it For example, we may suppose some vague desire in sightless animals to be able to be aware of objects before they were in contact with them This led to efforts which finally resulted in the creation of eyes Sight satisfied the desire, but could not have been imagined beforehand. For this reason, evolution is unpredictable, and determinism cannot refute the advocates of free will

This broad outline is filled in by an account of the actual development of life on the earth The first division of the current was into plants and animals plants aimed at storing up energy in a reservoir, animals aimed at using energy for sudden and rapid movements " The same impetus," he says, " that has led the animal to give itself nerves and nerve centres must have ended, in the plant, in the chlorophyllian function " (*C. E.*, p. 120) But among animals, at a later stage, a new bifurcation appeared *instinct* and *intellect* became more or less separated They are never wholly without each other, but in the main intellect is the misfortune of man, while instinct is seen at its best in ants, bees, and Bergson. The division between intellect and instinct is fundamental in his philosophy, much of which is a kind of Sandford and Merton, with instinct as the good boy and intellect as the bad boy

Instinct at its best is called *intuition*. " By *intuition*,"

4

he says, "I mean instinct that has become disinterested, selfconscious, capable of reflecting upon its object and of enlarging it indefinitely" (C. E , p. 186). The account of the doings of intellect is not always easy to follow, but if we are to understand Bergson we must do our best.

Intelligence or intellect, "as it leaves the hands of nature, has for its chief object the inorganic solid" (C. E , p. 162) ; it can only form a clear idea of the discontinuous and the immobile (pp 163-4) ; its concepts are outside each other like objects in space, and have the same stability (p. 169). The intellect separates in space and fixes in time ; it is not made to think evolution, but represent *becoming* as a series of states (p. 171) " The intellect is characterised by a natural inability to understand life " (p. 174) ; geometry and logic, which are its typical products, are strictly applicable to solid bodies, but elsewhere reasoning must be checked by common sense, which, as Bergson truly says, is a very different thing (p. 170) Solid bodies, it would seem, are something which mind has created on purpose to apply intellect to them, much as it has created chess-boards in order to play chess on them The genesis of intellect and the genesis of material bodies, we are told, are correlative : both have been developed by reciprocal adaptation (p 196). "An identical process must have cut out matter and the intellect, at the same time, from a stuff that contained both " (p 210).

This conception of the simultaneous growth of matter and intellect is ingenious, and deserves to be understood. Broadly, I think, what is meant is this Intellect is the power of seeing things as separate one from another, and matter is that which is separated into distinct things In reality there are no separate solid things, only an endless stream of becoming, in which nothing becomes and there is nothing that this nothing becomes. But becoming may be a move-ment up or a movement down . when it is a movement up it is called life, when it is a movement down it is what, as misapprehended by the intellect, is called matter. I suppose the universe is shaped like a cone, with the Absolute at the vertex, for the movement up brings things together, while the movement down separates them, or at least seems to do so. In order that the upward motion of mind may be able to thread its way through the downward motion of the falling bodies which hail upon it, it must be able to cut out paths between them, thus as intelligence was formed, outlines and paths appeared (p 199), and the primitive flux was cut up into separate bodies The intellect may be compared to a carver, but it has the peculiarly of imagining that the chicken was always the separate pieces into which the carving-knife divides it.

"The intellect," Bergson says, "always behaves as if it were fascinated by the contemplation of inert matter. It is life looking outward, putting itself outside itself, adopting the ways of inorganised nature in principle, in order to direct them in fact " (p 170) If we may be allowed to add another image to the many by which Bergson's philosophy is illustrated, we may say tnat the universe is a vast funicular railway, in which life is the train that goes up, and matter is the train that goes down The intellect consists in watching the descending train as it passes the ascending train in which we are. The obviously nobler faculty which concentrates its attention on our own train, is instinct or intuition It is possible to leap from one train to the other ; this happens when we become the victims of automatic habit, and is the essence of the comic. Or we can divide ourselves into parts, one part going up and one down, then only the part going down is comic. But intellect is not itself a descending motion, it is merely an observation of the descending motion by the ascending motion.

Intellect, which separates things, is, according to Bergson, a kind of dream ; it is not *active*, as all our life ought to be, but purely contemplative When we dream, he says, our self is scattered, our past is broken into fragments (p. 212),*

---

* It is noteworthy that elsewhere Bergson speaks of dreams as giving us duration more pure than in waking life (*T. and F.W.*, p 126).

things which really interpenetrate each other are seen
as separate solid units : the extra-spatial degrades itself into
spatiality (p, 218), which is nothing but separateness   Thus
all intellect, since it separates, tends to geometry, and logic,
which deals with concepts that lie wholly outside each other,
is really an outcome of geometry, following the direction of
materiality (pp 222-4)   Both deduction and induction
require spatial intuition behind them (p 225) ; " the movement at the end of which is spatiality lays down along its course
the faculty of induction, as well as that of deduction, in fact,
intellectuality entire."   It creates them in mind, and also
the order in things which the intellect finds there (p. 228).
Thus logic and mathematics do not represent a positive
spiritual effort (p 224), but a mere somnambulism, in which
the will is suspended, and the mind is no longer active   In-
capacity for mathematics is therefore a sign of grace—
fortunately a very common one

As intellect is connected with space, so instinct or intuition is connected with time.   It is one of the noteworthy
features of Bergson's philosophy that, unlike most writers,
he regards time and space as profoundly dissimilar.   Space,
the characteristic of matter, arises from a dissection of the
flux which is really illusory, useful, up to a certain point,
in practice, but utterly misleading in theory.   Time, on the
contrary, is the essential characteristic of life or mind.
" Wherever anything lives," he says, " there is, open somewhere, a register in which time is being inscribed " (*C. E.*,
p. 17).   But the time here spoken of is not mathematical
time, the homogeneous assemblage of mutually external
instants   Mathematical time, according to Bergson, is really
a form of space ; the time which is of the essence of life is
what he calls *duration*.   This conception of duration is fundamental in his philosophy ; it appears already in his earliest
book *Time and Free Will*, and it is necessary to understand
it if we are to have any comprehension of his system.   It
is, however, a very difficult conception   I do not fully under-

stand it myself, and therefore I cannot hope to explain it with all the lucidity which it doubtless deserves.

" Pure duration," we are told, " is the form which our conscious states assume when our ego lets itself *live*, when it refrains from separating its present state from its former states " (*T. and F W*, p 100) It forms the past and the present into one organic whole, where there is mutual penetration, succession without distinction (*ib*) " Within our ego, there is succession without mutual externality ; outside the ego, in pure space, there is mutual externality without succession " (p 108)

" Questions relating to subject and object, to their distinction and their union, should be put in terms of time rather than of space " (*M and M*, p 77) In the duration in which we *see ourselves acting*, there are dissociated elements ; but in the duration in which we *act*, our states melt into each other (*M and M.*, p. 243) Pure duration is what is most removed from externality and least penetrated with externality, a duration in which the past is big with a present absolutely new But then our will is strained to the utmost ; we have to gather up the past which is slipping away, and thrust it whole and undivided into the present At such moments we truly possess ourselves, but such moments are rare (*C. E.*, pp. 210-211) Duration is the very stuff of reality, which is perpetual becoming, never something made (*C E.*, p. 287)

It is above all in *memory* that duration exhibits itself, for in memory the past survives in the present. Thus the theory of memory becomes of great importance in Bergson's philosophy. *Matter and Memory* is concerned to show the relation of mind and matter, of which both are affirmed to be real (p. vii), by an analysis of memory, which is " just the intersection of mind and matter " (p. xii)

There are, to begin with, two radically different things, both of which are commonly called *memory ;* the clear distinction between these two is one of the best things in Bergson. " The past survives," he says, " under two distinct forms :

first, in motor mechanisms ; secondly, in independent recollections " (*M. and M.*, p. 87). For example, a man is said to
remember a poem if he can repeat it by heart, that is to say,
if he has acquired a certain habit or mechanism enabling him
to repeat a former action. But he might, at least theoretically,
be able to repeat the poem without any recollection of the
previous occasions on which he has read it ; thus there is no
consciousness of past events involved in this sort of memory.
The second sort, which alone really deserves to be called
memory, is exhibited in recollections of separate occasions
when he has read the poem, each unique and with a date.
Here there can be no question of *habit*, since each event only
occurred once, and had to make its impression immediately.
It is suggested that in some way everything that has happened
to us is remembered, but as a rule, only what is useful comes
into consciousness. Apparent failures of memory, it is argued,
are not really failures of the mental part of memory, but of
the motor mechanism for bringing memory into action This
view is supported by a discussion of brain physiology and the
facts of amnesia, from which it is held to result that true
memory is not a function of the brain (*M. and M.*, p. 315).
The past must be *acted* by matter, *imagined* by mind (*M. and
M.*, p 298) Memory is not an emanation of matter ; indeed
the contrary would be nearer the truth if we mean matter as
grasped in concrete perception, which always occupies a
certain duration (*M. and M.*, p. 237)

"Memory must be, in principle, a power absolutely
independent of matter. If, then, spirit is a reality, it is here,
in the phenomena of memory, that we may come into touch
with it experimentally " (*M. and M* , p. 81).

At the opposite end from pure memory Bergson places
pure perception, in regard to which he adopts an ultra-realist
position " In pure perception," he says, " we are actually
placed outside ourselves, we touch the reality of the object
in an immediate intuition " (p. 84). So completely does he
identify perception with its object that he almost refuses to
call it mental at all " Pure perception," he says, " which

is the lowest degree of mind—mind without memory—is really part of matter, as we understand matter " (*M. and M* , p 297) Pure perception is constituted by dawning action, its actuality lies in its activity (*M. and M* , p 74). It is in this way that the *brain* becomes relevant to perception, for the brain is not an instrument of representation, but an instrument of action (*M and M* , p 83) The function of the brain is to limit our mental life to what is practically useful. But for the brain, one gathers, everything would be perceived, but in fact we only perceive what interests us (cf *M and M* , p. 34) " The body, always turned towards action, has for its essential function to limit, with a view to action, the life of the spirit " (*M and M* , p 233) It is, in fact, an instrument of choice

We must now return to the subject of instinct or intuition, as opposed to intellect. It was necessary first to give some account of duration and memory, since Bergson's theories of duration and memory are presupposed in his account of intuition In man, as he now exists, intuition is the fringe or penumbra of intellect it has been thrust out of the centre by being less useful in action than intellect, but it has deeper uses which make it desirable to bring it back into greater prominence Bergson wishes to make intellect " turn inwards on itself, and awaken the potentialities of intuition which still slumber within it " (*C E* , p 192) The relation between instinct and intellect is compared to that between sight and touch Intellect, we are told, will not give knowledge of things at a distance ; indeed the function of science is said to be to explain all perceptions in terms of touch

" Instinct alone," he says, " is knowledge at a distance It has the same relation to intelligence that vision has to touch " (*C E* , p 177) We may observe in passing that, as appears in many passages, Bergson is a strong visualiser, whose thought is always conducted by means of visual images. Many things which he declares to be necessities of all thought are, I believe, characteristic of visualisers, and would not be true of those who think by means of auditory images He always exalts the sense of sight at the expense of the other senses, and his views on space would seem to be largely determined by this fact. I shall return to this question at a later stage.

The essential characteristic of intuition is that it does not divide the world into separate things, as the intellect does, although Bergson does not use these words, we might describe it as synthetic rather than analytic   It apprehends a multiplicity, but a multiplicity of interpenetrating processes, not of spatially external bodies   There are in truth no *things* : : " things and states are only views, taken by our mind, of becoming. There are no things, there are only actions " (*C. E.*, p. 261)   This view of the world, which appears difficult and unnatural to intellect, is easy and natural to intuition. Memory affords an instance of what is meant, for in memory the past lives on into the present and interpenetrates it.   Apart from mind, the world would be perpetually dying and being born again ; the past would have no reality, and therefore there would be no past.   It is memory, with its correlative desire, that makes the past and the future real and therefore creates true duration and true time.   Intuition alone can understand this mingling of past and future : to the intellect they remain external, spatially external as it were, to one another.   Under the guidance of intuition, we perceive that " form is only a snapshot view of a transition " (*C. E.*, p. 319), and the philosopher " will see the material world melt back into a single flux " (*C. E*, p 390).

Closely connected with the merits of intuition is Bergson's doctrine of freedom and his praise of action   " In reality," he says, " a living being is a centre of action   It represents a certain sum of contingency entering into the world, that is to say, a certain quantity of possible action " (*C E.*, p 276). The arguments against free will depend partly upon assuming that the intensity of psychical states is a *quantity*, capable, at least in theory, of numerical measurement ; this view Bergson undertakes to refute in the first chapter of *Time and Free Will*. Partly the determinist depends, we are told, upon a confusion

between true duration and mathematical time, which Bergson regards as really a form of space Partly, again, the determinist rests his case upon the unwarranted assumption that, when the state of the brain is given, the state of the mind is theroretically determinate Bergson is willing to admit that the converse is true that is to say, that the state of brain is determinate when the state of mind is given, but he regards the mind as more differentiated than the brain, and therefore holds that many different states of mind may correspond to one state of brain He concludes that real freedom is possible :
" We are free when our acts spring from our whole personality, when they express it, when they have that indefinable resemblance to it which one sometimes finds between the artist and his work " (*T. and F W.*, p 172)

In the above outline, I have in the main endeavoured merely to state Bergson's views, without giving the reasons adduced by him in favour of their truth This is easier than it would be with most philosophers, since as a rule he does not give reasons for his opinions, but relies on their inherent attractiveness, and on the charm of an excellent style Like the advertisers of Oxo. he relies upon picturesque and varied statement, and an apparent explanation of many obscure facts. Analogies and similes, especially form a very large part of the whole process by which he recommends his views to the reader. The number of similes for life to be found in his works exceeds the number in any poet known to me. Life, he says, is like a shell bursting into fragments which are again shells (*C E.*, p 103) It is like a sheaf (*ib*, p 104) Initially, it was " a tendency to accumulate in a reservoir, as do especially the green parts of vegetables " (*ib*, p 260). But the reservoir is to be filled with boiling water from which steam is issuing ; " jets must be gushing out unceasingly, of which each, falling back, is a world " (*ib.*, p 261). Again, " life appears in its entirety as an immense wave which, starting from a centre, spreads outwards, and which on almost the whole of its circumference is stopped and converted into oscillation : at one single point the obstacle has been forced,

the impulsion has passed freely " (*ib* , p. 280)   Then there is
the great climax in which life is compared to a cavalry charge.
" All organised beings, from the humblest to the highest,
from the first origins of life to the time in which we are, and
in all places as in all times, do but evidence a single impulsion,
the inverse of the movement of matter, and in itself indivisible.
All the living hold together, and all yield to the same
tremendous push   The animal takes its stand on the plant,
man best rides animality, and the whole of humanity, in space
and in time, is one immense army galloping beside and before
and behind each of us in an overwhelming charge able to beat
down every resistance and to clear many obstacles, perhaps
even death " (*C. E.*, pp 285-6)

But a cool critic, who feels himself a mere spectator,
perhaps an unsympathetic spectator, of the charge in which
man is mounted upon animality, may be inclined to think
that calm and careful thought is hardly compatible with
this form of exercise.   When he is told that thought is a
mere means of action, the mere impulse to avoid obstacles
in the field, he may feel that such a view is becoming in a
cavalry officer, but not in a philosopher, whose business, after
all, is with thought : he may feel that in the passion and noise
of violent motion there is no room for the fainter music of
reason, no leisure for the disinterested contemplation in which
greatness is sought, not by turbulence, but by the greatness
of the universe which is mirrored.   In that case, he may be
tempted to ask whether there are any reasons for accepting
such a restless view of the world   And if he asks this question,
he will find, if I am not mistaken, that there is no reason
whatever for accepting this view, either in the universe or in
the writings of M. Bergson

II.

The two foundations of Bergson's philosophy, in so far
as it is more than an imaginative and poetic view of the
world, are his doctrines of space and time   His doctrine of
space is required for his condemnation of the intellect, and

if he fails in his condemnation of the intellect, the intellect will succeed in its condemnation of him, for between the two it is war to the knife. His doctrine of time is necessary for his vindication of freedom, for his escape from what William James called a " block universe," for his doctrine of a perpetual flux in which there is nothing that flows, and for his whole account of the relations between mind and matter. It will be well, therefore, in criticism, to concentrate on these two doctrines If they are true, such minor errors and incon- sistencies as no philosopher escapes would not greatly matter, while if they are false, nothing remains except an imaginative epic, to be judged on esthetic rather than on intellectual grounds I shall begin with the theory of space, as being the simpler of the two

Bergson's theory of space occurs fully and explicitly in his *Time and Free Will*, and therefore belongs to the oldest parts of his philosophy In his first chapter, he contends that *greater* and *less* imply space, since he regards the greater as essentially that which *contains* the less He offers no argume its whatever, either good or bad, in favour of this view ; he merely exclaims, as though he were giving an obvious *reductio ad absurdum* . " As if one could still speak of magni- tude where there is neither multiplicity nor space ! " (p. 9). The obvious cases to the contrary, such as pleasure and pain, afford him much difficulty, yet he never doubts or re-examines the dogma with which he starts.

In his next chapter, he maintains the same thesis as regards number. " As soon as we wish to picture *number* to ourselves," he says, " and not merely figures or words, we are compelled to have recourse to an extended image " (p. 78), and " every clear idea of number implies a visual image in space " (p 79) These two sentences suffice to show, as I shall try to prove, that Bergson does not know what number is, and has himself no clear idea of it. This is shown also by his definition : " Number may be defined in general as a collection of units, or, speaking more exactly, as the synthesis of the one and the many " (p. 75).

In discussing these statements, I must ask the reader's patience for a moment while I call attention to some distinctions which may at first appear pedantic, but are really vital. There are three entirely different things which are confused by Bergson in the above statements, namely · (1) number, the general concept applicable to the various particular numbers , (2) the various particular numbers , (3) the various collections to which the various particular numbers are applicable   It is this last that is defined by Bergson when he says that number is a collection of units   The twelve apostles, the twelve tribes of Israel, the twelve months, the twelve signs of the zodiac, are all collections of units, yet no one of them is the number 12, still less is it number in general, as by the above definition it ought to be   The number 12, obviously, is something which all these collections have in common but which they do not have in common with other collections, such as cricket elevens   Hence the number 12 is neither a collection of twelve terms, nor is it something which all collections have in common ; and number in general is a property of 12 or 11 or any other number, but not of the various collections that have twelve terms or eleven terms

Hence when, following Bergson's advice, we " have recourse to an extended image " and picture, say, twelve dots such as are obtained by throwing double sixes at dice, we have still not obtained a picture of the number 12   The number 12, in fact, is something more abstract than any picture.   Before we can be said to have any understanding of the number 12, we must know what different collections of twelve units have in common, and this is something which cannot be pictured because it is abstract   Bergson only succeeds in making his theory of number plausible by confusing a particular collection with the number of its terms, and this again with number in general.

The confusion is the same as if we confused a particular young man with youth, and youth with the general concept " period of human life," and were then to argue that because a young man has two legs, youth must have two legs, and the general concept " period of human life " must have two legs. The confusion is important because, as soon as it is perceived, the theory that number or particular numbers can be pictured in space is seen to be untenable This not only disproves Bergson's theory as to number, but also his more general theory that all abstract ideas and all logic are derived from space , for the abstract 12, the common property of all dozens as opposed to any particular dozen, though it is never present to his mind, is obviously conceivable and obviously incapable of being pictured in space

But apart from the question of numbers, shall we admit Bergson's contention that every plurality of separate units involves space ? Some of the cases that appear to contradict this view are corsidered by him, for example successive sounds When we hear the steps of a passer-by in the street, he says, we visualise his successive positions , when we hear the strokes of a bell, we either picture it swinging backwards and forwards, or we range the successive sounds in an ideal space (T and F W , p 86) But these are mere autobio-graphical observations of a visualiser, and illustrate the remark we made before, that Bergson's views depend upon the predominance of the sense of sight in him There is no logical necessity to range the strokes of a clock in an imaginary space most people, I imagine, count them without any spatial auxiliary Yet no reason is alleged by Bergson for the view that space is necessary He assumes this as obvious, and proceeds at once to apply it to the case of times Where there seem to be different times outside each other, he says, the times are pictured as spread out in space ; in real time, such as is given by memory, different times interpenetrate each other, and cannot be counted because they are not separate

The view that all separateness implies space is now supposed established, and is used deductively to prove that space is involved wherever there is obviously separateness however little other reason there may be for suspecting such a thing. Thus abstract ideas, for example, obviously exclude each other whiteness is different from blackness, health is different from sickness, folly is different from wisdom   Hence all abstract ideas involve space ; and therefore logic, which uses abstract ideas, is an offshot of geometry, and the whole of the intellect depends upon a supposed habit of picturing things side by side in space   This conclusion, upon which Bergson's whole condemnation of the intellect rests, is based, so far as can be discovered, entirely upon a personal idiosyncrasy mistaken for a necessity of thought, I mean the idiosyncrasy of visualising successions as spread out on a line. The instance of numbers shows that, if Bergson were in the right, we could never have attained to the abstract ideas which are supposed to be thus impregnated with space ; and conversely, the fact that we can understand abstract ideas (as opposed to particular things which exemplify them) seems sufficient to prove that he is wrong in regarding the intellect as impregnated with space

One of the bad effects of an anti-intellectual philosophy, such as that of Bergson, it that it thrives upon the errors and confusions of the intellect. Hence it is led to prefer bad thinking to good, to declare every momentary difficulty insoluble, and to regard every foolish mistake as revealing the bankruptcy of intellect and the triumph of intuition. There are in Bergson's works many allusions to mathematics and science, and to a careless reader these allusions may seem to strengthen his philosophy greatly   As regards science, especially biology and physiology, I am not competent to criticise his interpretations. But as regards mathematics, he has deliberately preferred traditional errors in interpretation to the more modern views which have prevailed among mathematicians for the last half century. In this matter, he has followed the example of most philosophers. In the eighteenth and early nineteenth centuries, the infinitesimal calculus, though well developed as a method, was supported, as regards its foundations, by many fallacies and much confused thinking. Hegel and his followers seized upon these fallacies and confusions, to support them in their attempt to prove all mathematics self-contradictory. Thence the Hegelian account of these matters passed into the current thought of philosophers, where it has remained long after the mathematicians have removed all the difficulties upon which the philosophers rely. And so long as the main object of philosophers is to show that nothing can be learned by patience and detailed thinking, but that we ought rather to worship the prejudices of the ignorant under the title of "reason" if we are Hegelians, or of "intuition" if we are Bergsonians, so long philosophers will take care to remain ignorant of what mathematicians have done to remove the errors by which Hegel profited.

Apart from the question of number which we have already considered, the chief point at which Bergson touches mathematics is his rejection of what he calls the "cinematographic" representation of the world Mathematics conceives change, even continuous change, as constituted by a series of states ; Bergson, on the contrary, contends that no series of states can represent what is continuous, and that in change a thing is never in any state at all This view that change is constituted by a series of changing states he calls cinematographic , this view, he says, is natural to the intellect, but is radically vicious. True change can only be explained by true duration ; it involves an interpenetration of past and present, not a mathematical succession of static states. This is what is called a "dynamic" instead of a "static" view of the world. The question is important, and in spite of its difficulty we cannot pass it by.

Bergson's position is illustrated—and what is to be said in criticism may also be aptly illustrated—by Zeno's argument of the arrow Zeno argues that, since the arrow at each moment simply is where it is, thereforethe arrow in its flight is always at rest. At first sight, this argument may not appear a very powerful one Of course, it will be said, the arrow is where it is at one moment, but at another moment it is somewhere else, and this is just was constitutes motion.

Certain difficulties, it is true, arise out of the continuity of motion, if we insist upon assuming that motion is also dis-continuous. These difficulties, thus obtained, have long been part of the stock-in-trade of philosophers. But if, with the mathematicians, we avoid the assumption that motion is also discontinuous, we shall not fall into the philosopher's difficulties. A cinematograph in which there are an infinite number of films, and in which there is never a *next* film because an infinite number come between any two, will perfectly represent a continuous motion. Wherein, then, lies the force of Zeno's argument ?

Zeno belonged to the Eleatic school, whose object was to prove that there could be no such thing as change. The natural view to take of the world is that there are *things* which *change* ; for example, there is an arrow which is now here, now there By bisection of this view, philosophers have developed two paradoxes The Eleatics said that there were things but no changes , Heraclitus and Bergson said that there were changes but no things The Eleatics said there was an arrow, but no flight ; Heraclitus and Bergson said there was a flight but no arrow. Each party conducted its argument by refutation of the other party. How ridiculous to say there is no arrow ' say the " static " party. How ridiculous to say there is no flight ' say the " dynamic " party The unfortunate man who stands in the middle and maintains that there is both the arrow and its flight is assumed by the disputants to deny both , he is therefore pierced, like St Sebastian, by the arrow from one side and by its flight from the other. But we have still not discovered wherein lies the force of Zeno's argument.

Zeno assumes, tacitly, the essence of the Bergsonian theory of change That is to say, he assumes that when a thing is in a process of continuous change, even if it is only change of position, there must be in the thing some internal *state* of change. The thing must, at each instant, be in-trinsically different from what it would be if it were not changing. He then points out that at each instant the arrow

simply is where it is, just as it would be if it were at rest.
Hence he concludes that there can be no such thing as a *state*
of motion, and therefore, adhering to the view that a state of
motion is essential to motion, he infers that there can be no
motion and that the arrow is always at rest

Zeno's argument, therefore, though it does not touch
the mathematical account of change, does, *prima facie*,
refute a view of change which is not unlike M Bergson's
How, then, does M Bergson meet Zeno's argument ? He
meets it by denying that the arrow is ever anywhere. After
stating Zeno's argument, he replies · " Yes, if we suppose
that the arrow can ever *be* in a point of its course. Yes
again, if the arrow, which is moving, ever coincides with a
position, which is motionless But the arrow never *is* in
any point of its course " (*C. E.*, p. 325). This reply to Zeno,
or a closely similar one concerning Achilles and the Tortoise,
occurs in all his three books Bergson's view, plainly, is
paradoxical , whether it is *possible*, is a question which
demands a discussion of his view of duration. His only argument in its favour is the statement that the mathematical
view of change " implies the absurd proposition that movement is made of immobilities " (*C. E*, p 325) But the
apparent absurdity of this view is merely due to the verbal
form in which he has stated it, and vanishes as soon as we
realise that motion implies relations A friendship, for
example, is made out of people who are friends, but not out of
friendships ; a genealogy is made out of men, but not out of
genealogies So a motion is made out of what is moving,
but not out of motions It expresses the fact that a thing
may be in different places at different times, and that the places
may still be different, however near together the times may
be. Bergson's argument against the mathematical view of
motion, therefore, reduces itself, in the last analysis, to a mere
play upon words And with this conclusion we may pass
on to a criticism of his theory of duration.

Bergson's theory of duration is bound up with his theory
of memory. According to this theory, things remembered

survive in memory, and thus interpenetrate present things : past and present are not mutually external, but are mingled in the unity of consciousness. Action, he says, is what constitutes being ; but mathematical time is a mere passive receptacle, which does nothing and therefore is nothing (*C. E.*, p. 41). The past, he says, is that which acts no longer, and the present is that which is acting (*M and M.*, p. 74). But in this statement, as indeed throughout his account of duration, Bergson is unconsciously assuming the ordinary mathematical time , without this, his statements are unmeaning. What is meant by saying " the past is essentially *that which acts no longer* " (his italics), except that the past is that of which the action is past ? The words " no longer " are words expressive of the past ; to a person who did not have the ordinary notion of the past as something outside the present, these words would have no meaning Thus his definition is circular. What he says is, in effect, " the past is that of which the action is in the past." As a definition, this cannot be regarded as a happy effort. And the same applies to the present. The present, we are told, is " *that which is acting* " (his italics) * But the word " is " introduces just that idea of the present which was to be defined. The present is that which *is* acting as opposed to that which *was* acting or *will be* acting. That is to say, the present is that whose action is in the present, not in the past or in the future. Again the definition is circular. An earlier passage on the same page will illustrate the fallacy further. " That which constitutes our pure perception," he says, " is our dawning action . . . The *actuality* of our perception thus lies in its *activity*, in the movements which prolong it, and not in its greater intensity . the past is only idea, the present is ideo-motor " (*ib*) This passage makes it quite clear that, when Bergson speaks of the past, he does not mean the past,

---

* Similarly in *Matter and Memory* (p 193) he says it is a question whether the past has ceased to exist, or has only *ceased* to be useful. The present, he says, is not that which is, but that which *is being made* The words I have italicized here really involve the usual view of time

but our present memory of the past. The past when it existed was just as active as the present is now ; if Bergson's account were correct, the present moment ought to be the only one in the whole history of the world containing any activity

In earlier times there were other perceptions, just as active, just as actual in their day, as our present perception , the past, in its day, was by no means only idea, but was in its intrinsic character just what the present is now   This real past, however, Bergson simply forgets , what he speaks of is the present idea of the past.   The real past does not mingle with the present   Our memory of the past does of course mingle with the present, since it is part of it , but that is a very different thing.

The whole of Bergson's theory of duration and time rests throughout on the elementary confusion between the present occurrence of a recollection and the past occurrence which is recollected   But for the fact that time is so familiar to us, the vicious circle involved in his attempt to deduce the past as what is no longer active would be obvious at once.   As it is, what Bergson gives is an account of the difference between perception and recollection—both *present* facts—and what he believes himself to have given is an account of the difference between the present and the past. As soon as this confusion is realised, his theory of time is seen to be simply a theory which omits time altogether

The confusion between present remembering and the past event remembered, which seems to be at the bottom of Bergson's theory of time, is an instance of a more general confusion which, if I am not mistaken, vitiates a great deal of his thought, and indeed a great deal of the thought of most modern philosophers—I mean the confusion between an act of knowing and that which is known   In memory, the act of knowing is in the present, whereas what is known is in the past ; thus by confusing them the distinction between past and present is blurred.   In perception, the act of knowing is mental, whereas what is known is (at least in one sense) physical or material ; thus by confusing the two, the distinction between mind and matter is blurred. This enables Bergson to say, as we saw, that "pure perception, which is the lowest degree of mind . . is really part of matter." The act of perceiving is mind, while that which is perceived is (in one sense) matter ; thus when these two are confused, the above statement becomes intelligible.

Throughout *Matter and Memory*, this confusion between the act of knowing and the object known is indispensable. It is enshrined in the use of the word "image," which is explained at the very beginning of the book.* He there states that, apart from philosophical theories, everything that we know consists of "images," which indeed constitute the whole universe He says "I call *matter* the aggregate of images, and *perception of matter* these same images referred to the eventual action of one particular image, my body " (*M. and M.*, p 8). It will be observed that matter and the perception of matter, according to him, consist of the very same things. The brain, he says, is like the rest of the material universe, and is therefore an image if the universe is an image (p. 9).

Since the brain, which nobody sees, is not, in the ordinary. sense, an image, we are not surprised at his saying that an image can *be* without *being perceived* (p 27) ; but he explains later on that, as regards images, the difference between *being* and *being consciously perceived* is only one of degree (p. 30). This is perhaps explained by another passage in which he says . "What can be a non-perceived material object, an image not imaged, unless it is a kind of unconscious mental state ? " (p. 183) Finally (p. 304) he says "That every reality has a kinship, an analogy, in short a relation with consciousness—this is what we concede to idealism by the very fact that we term things 'images.' " Nevertheless he attempts to allay our initial doubt by saying that he is begin-

---

* Bergson's use of the word "image" is made clearer by a very penetrating analysis of Berkeley in a recent article, "L'Intuition Philosophique" (*Revue de Metaphysique et de Morale,* Nov. 1911). This article displays very distinctly the profound influence of Berkeley on Bergson's thought Bergson's "image" is practically Berkeley's " idea "

ning at a point before any of the assumptions of philosophers have been introduced. " We will assume," he says, " for the moment that we know nothing of theories of matter and theories of spirit, nothing of the discussions as to the reality or ideality of the external world   Here I am in the presence of images " (p   I)   And in the new Introduction which he wrote for the English edition he says . " By ' image ' we mean a certain existence which is more than that which the idealist calls a *representation*, but less than that which the realist calls a *thing*—an existence placed halfway between the ' thing ' and the ' representation ' " (p vii.).

The distinction which Bergson has in mind in the above is not, I think, the distinction between the imaging as a mental occurrence and the thing imaged as an object   He is thinking of the distinction between the thing as it is and the thing as it appears, neither of which belongs to the subject   The distinction between subject and object, between the mind which thinks and remembers and has images on the one hand, and the objects thought about, remembered, or imaged— this distinction, so far as I can see, is wholly absent from his philosophy   Its absence is his real debt to idealism , and a very unfortunate debt it is   In the case of " images," as we have just seen, it enables him first to speak of images as neutral between mind and matter, then to assert that the brain is an image in spite of the fact that it has never been imaged, then to suggest that matter and the perception of matter are the same thing, but that a non-perceived image (such as the brain) is an unconscious mental state ; while finally, the use of the word " image," though involving no metaphysical theories whatever, nevertheless implies that every reality has " a kinship, an analogy, in short a relation " with consciousness.

All these confusions are due to the initial confusion of subject and object   The subject—a thought or an image or a memory—is a present fact in me , the object may be the law of gravitation or my friend Jones or the old Campanile of Venice   The subject is mental and is here and now   Therefore, if subject and object are one, the object is mental and is here and now : my friend Jones, though he believes himself to be in South America and to exist on his own account, is really in my head and exists in virtue of my thinking about him ; St. Mark's Campanile, in spite of its great size and the fact that it ceased to exist ten years ago, still exists, and is to be found complete inside me   These statements are no travesty of Bergson's theories of space and time ; they are merely an attempt to show what is the actual concrete meaning of those theories

The confusion of subject and object is not peculiar to Bergson, but is common to many idealists and many materialists. Many idealists say that the object is really the subject, and many materialists say that the subject is really the object. They agree in thinking these two statements very different, while yet holding that subject and object are not different. In this respect, we may admit, Bergson has merit, for he is as ready impartially to identify subject with object as to identify object with subject   As soon as this identification is rejected, his whole system collapses : first his theories of space and time, then his belief in real contingency, then his condemnation of intellect, then his account of the relations of mind and matter, and last of all his whole view that the universe contains no things, but only actions, movements, changes, from nothing to nothing, in an endless alternation of up and down

Of course a large part of Bergson's philosophy, probably the part to which most of its popularity is due, does not depend upon argument, and cannot be upset by argument. His imaginative picture of the world, regarded as a poetic effort, is in the main not capable of either proof or disproof. Shakespeare says life's but a walking shadow, Shelley says it is like a dome of many coloured glass, Bergson says it is a shell which bursts into parts that are again shells. If you like Bergson's image better, it is just as legitimate.

The good which Bergson hopes to see realised in the world is action for the sake of action. All pure contemplation he calls "dreaming," and condemns by a whole series of uncomplimentary epithets static, Platonic, mathematical, logical, intellectual   Those who desire some prevision of the end which action is to achieve are told that an end foreseen would be nothing new, because desire, like memory, is identified with its object   Thus we are condemned, in action, to be the blind slaves of instinct   the life-force pushes us on from behind, restlessly and unceasingly   There is no room in this philosophy for the moment of contemplative insight when, rising above the animal life, we become conscious of the greater ends that redeem man from the life of the brutes Those to whom activity without purpose seems a sufficient good will find in Bergson's books a pleasing picture of the univers . But those to whom action, if it is to be of any value, must be inspired by some vision, by some imaginative fore-shadowing of a world less painful, less unjust, less full of strife than the world of our every-day life, those, in a word, whose action is built on contemplation, will find in this philosophy nothing of what they seek, and will not regret that there is no reason to think it true

ON MR. RUSSELL'S REASONS FOR SUPPOSING THAT BERGSON'S PHILOSOPHY IS NOT TRUE

BY H. WILDON CARR.

In his criticism of Bergson, Mr. Russell begins by giving a description of Bergson's philosophy which presents the leading features of the doctrine, with certain ironical touches such as we expect from " a cool ciitic, who feels himself a spectator, perhaps an unsympathetic spectator," and concludes with the opinion that there is no reason whatever for accepting it, either in the universe or in the writings of Mr. Bergson   Had Mr Russell ended his paper with this negative conclusion, he would have thrown on the champion of Bergson, willing to take up the challenge, the formidable task of discovering a reason that would oblige the critic to modify his attitude, but fortunately in the second part of his paper he has given us two reasons for rejecting the philosophy.   It is these two reasons that seem to me to demand careful examination and reply.

The two reasons are directed against the two foundations of Bergson's philosophy, the doctrines of space and of time. In singling out these points for his attack, Mr. Russell has shown something like the anatomical skill of the paralysing wasp in one of Bergson's best known illustrations ; if the argument gets home, it will destroy all power for harm the philosophy may have without killing it outright, for Mr. Russell is willing to leave us its poetry

The first argument is directed against the well known and fundamental doctrine that the intellect is a mode of activity whose essential function is to spatialise reality.   Whatever the object that we apprehend intellectually, becomes in such

intellectual apprehension an extended image Mr. Russell
takes the particular instance of number and proceeds to prove
that Bergson does not know what number is, and has himself
no clear idea of it   Three entirely different things are confused, he tells us, in Bergson's account namely, (1) number,
the general concept applicable to the various particular
numbers, (2) the various particular numbers and (3) the
various collections to which the various particular numbers
are applicable. When, therefore, Bergson says that "as
soon as we wish to picture *number* to ourselves and not merely
figures or words, we are compelled to have recourse to an
extended image," this can only refer to meaning (3) and to
assert it of (1) or (2) shows a failure to appreciate a vital
distinction

Before I attempt to reply to this argument, let me clear
the ground by examining a suggested explanation that
Mr. Russell offers of the reason why Bergson may have failed
to understand this distinction, a reason of a personal and
psychological nature, namely, that Bergson is a visualizer
Mr Russell makes a great point of this   He suggests it first
of all in his general survey and then returns to it as something
illustrate i and demonstrated by this very case in point. When
Mr Russell says that Bergson is a visualizer he seems, indeed,
to suggest that to be a visualizer is to suffer from a defect
which distinctly handicaps the patient   We may be quite
sure that Mr Russell intends nothing of the kind if he did
we should be driven to suppose that he considered the only
person capable of pure appreciation of philosophical distinctions is the man blind from his birth   Psychologists divide
us all, I believe, according to the prevailing character of our
mental imagery, according to whether it is prevailingly visual,
auditory or motor, and it is found that we differ from one
another very considerably in this respect, but I do not know
that it has ever been alleged that one form of imagery rather
'than another either gives an intellectual advantage or constitutes an intellectual defect   But whether that is so or not,
anyone who has the psychological habit of introspection can

test for himself the prevailing character of his imagery and so can know whether he is or is not a visualizer, and if that is so I can settle the question finally so far as Bergson is concerned, for I have learnt on his own authority that he is not.

Of the meanings of number, Mr Russell allows that Bergson's doctrine that intellectual apprehension compels us to have recourse to an extended image is true of meaning (3) but denies tnat it is true of meanings (1) and (2). Here then is a clear issue It is important to note that Bergson himself in the sentence criticised makes a distinction " As soon as we wish to picture *number and not merely figures or words."* The italics are Bergson's. This is important because it admits that we can, and ordinarily do, apprehend meanings by figures or words and these do not compel recourse to an extended image " It is the clear idea of number that implies a visual image in space " It does not seem to me material to the argument that the image should be visual as distinct from auditory or motor, the essential thing is that it is spatial It should be borne in mind that Bergson uses the word image for what Mr. Russell calls a sense datum and other pnilosophers a presentation , and perhaps the greatest disadvantage of Bergson's term is that it suggests something exclusively visual Now Mr Russell has arranged his three meanings in a certain order,—is this oider also an order of knowing ? To be more precise, does Mr Russell hold that we can be acquainted with meaning (1) while totally un-acquainted with meaning (2) ? and meaning (2) while unacquainted with meaning (3). Let us see Mr Russell holds tnat we know universals and sense data by acquaintance, and also that the universal is an object of knowledge quite distinct from particular instances Thus the number 12 is a universal known by acquaintance, it is applicable to various particular instances, the twelve apostles, twelve tribes of Israel, &c , none of which instances is the number 12, but the number 12 is something common to all the instances, whether these are known or unknown, actual or possible, existent or non-existent. Suppose this granted, can we apprehend the number 12 if we have never had acquaintance with any particular instance of 12 units? Clearly Mr Russell's definition shows that this is impossible, and that there can only be acquaintance with a universal if there has already been acquaintance with sense data which are particular, for how does he define the number 12? "The number 12, obviously," he says, "is something which all these collections of 12 units have in common" Suppose then I am not acquainted with any collection of 12 units clearly I cannot be acquainted with that which is common to all collections of 12 units? Granting then that the universal, tne number 12 is a distinct object of tne mind, known by acquaintance, how can its meaning be apprehended except as " a synthesis of the one and many," and how can a synthesis be presented to the mind except by recourse to an extended image? But, says Mr. Russell, "we cannot picture the number 12 because it is something more abstract than any picture" No doubt, but to admit that it is more abstract than any picture is not to prove that we apprenend it without recourse to an extended image Let us grant that the abstract 12 "is obviously conceivable and obviously incapable of being pictured in space," we have still to acknowledge that this abstract 12 is "what different collections of 12 units have in common" We may not picture the abstract 12 but we are dependent on an extended image for our apprehension of its meaning Unless therefore Mr Russell holds that, like Condillac's statue with no sense but that of smell, there might exist a mind with no object present to it but the abstract 12, I for one see no reason in his argument for supposing Bergson's doctrine not true.

In close connection with this argument Mr. Russell charges Bergson with neglect of the modern views of mathematics. "He deliberately," he says, "preferred traditional errors in interpretation to the more modern views which have prevailed among mathematicians for the last half century." Now I am not qualified, and therefore shall not presume to discuss mathematical theories with Mr Russell, I go to him to learn, not to criticise I will look at this charge therefore from the standpoint of a disinterested spectator.

The case in point is Bergson's solution of Zeno's argument of the arrow According to Mr Russell, modern mathematics states the problem in terms that deprive the paradox of meaning, so that Zeno's problem no longer exists and Bergson's argument to meet it is superfluous This, Mr. Russell admits, is Zeno's fault, not Bergson's, but if Bergson had familiarised himself with modern mathematical theory he would not have revived the ancient puzzle. Let us put the two solutions side by side Bergson says that Zeno failed to see that a movement is indivisible, you can only divide it by stopping it, and that is destroying it, not dividing it You think you can divide it because you measure the course of the trajectory, and that being spatial, and therefore immobile, is divisible infinitely Modern mathematics, on the other hand, says that continuity is infinite divisibility, that is to say, that if there is an infinite number between any two numbers in a series, so that there is no next number, then the series is continuous—this is all that continuity can mean. " A cinematograph," says Mr Russell, " in which there are an infinite number of films, and in which there is never a *next* film, because an infinite number comes between any two, will perfectly represent a continuous motion " Well, of course, we must admit that, if we accept this definition of continuity it takes away the ground of Zeno's argument— but does it remove the paradox in the idea of movement ? This is the kind of difficulty I feel in regard to all Mr. Russell's work, he removes one paradox only to leave me with a greater. If I am puzzled to understand how Achilles can overtake the tortoise, Mr Russell leaves me in doubt whether I can even affirm that the tortoise cannot overtake Achilles. Is there not a one-to-one relation between the fast stride of Achilles and the slow step of the tortoise, so that, granted infinite time, every step that Achilles takes will be taken by the tortoise ?

Bergson may be right or he may be wrong, but he offers a solution of a paradox, whereas Mr. Russell offers a choice of paradoxes I, for one, can find no reason in modern views of mathematics for supposing the Bergson's solution is not true

I now come to the second fundamental position that Mr. Russell attacks, namely, Bergson's theory of duration This attack, if it succeeds, is the more deadly of the two. Here again it is a confusion of two things that are quite distinct that is charged against Bergson,—the confusion between the act of knowing and that which is known If this can be brought home to him then Mr Russell tells us " his whole system collapses first his theories of space and time, then his belief in real contingency, then his condemnation of intellect, then his account of the relation of mind and matter, and, last of all, his whole view that the universe contains no things but only actions, movements, changes from nothing to nothing, in an endless alternation of up and down." The phrase " nothing to nothing " in this quotation ignores the important and essential doctrine which Bergson insists is fundamental to the comprehension of his view, namely, that nothing is a pseudo-idea. It is also rather curious that Mr. Russell attributes the confusion he alleges between the act of knowing and that which is known, in part to the profound influence of Berkeley on Bergson's thought, whereas, Dr. Dawes Hicks, who has made the same criticism of Bergson, insists that this very distinction is clearly remarked by Berkeley and essential to the Berkeleyan view. This however by the way, our concern is to know if Mr Russell's charge is true I think the criticism simply rests on a failure to appreciate the exact problem that Bergson is dealing with in his doctrine of duration I do not know that Bergson has anywhere distinctly approached the problem of knowledge from the standpoint of what Meinong calls *Gegenstandstheorie.* I do not know what his view on that problem would be if he did give attention to it, but I cannot see its relevance to the actual doctrine of duration The distinction between the act of knowing and that which is known is surely implicit, if it is not explicit, in all that Bergson has said of intellectual knowledge   Has not Mr. Russell himself called our attention in this paper to Bergson's ultra-realist position in regard to perception ?   How is a confusion between subject and object consistent with any realist theory ?   It can only be with regard to the knowledge that Bergson calls intuition that this charge of confusion can have any semblance of meaning, and there so far from the identity of subject and object being a confusion it is of the very essence of the doctrine.   Mr. Russell is perfectly entitled to question or deny that we can have knowledge by intuition, but if there is such knowledge it is characterised by just this fact that it is consciousness of life in living   The act of knowing turns inwards, itself knows its knowing   Now we are all ready to admit that such knowledge is rare and very difficult, and Mr. Russell may be right if he holds that it is not merely difficult but impossible, but he has no right to charge Bergson with confusing two things which if this knowledge exists are identical, namely, the act of knowing and that which is known.

As I am one of those to whom not the poetry but only the metaphysics of Bergson makes appeal, I am glad that I do not find in either of Mr Russell's reasons a reason to think that this philosophy is not true.

MR WILDON CARR'S DEFENCE OF BERGSON

BY THE HON. BERTRAND RUSSELL

At the outset, it seems necessary to clear up a misconception of my purpose I did not attempt to prove that "Bergson's philosophy is not true," if we mean by his philosophy the conclusions at which he arrives rather than the reasons which he gives for them   The conclusion of the first part of my paper, quoted by Mr. Carr, is that " there is no reason whatever for accepting this view " ; the conclusion of the second part is almost verbally the same, namely " that there is no reason to think it true " These phrases were intentional. M Bergson's philosophy, like all other ambitious systems, is supported by arguments which I believe to be fallacious, but it does not follow that it is in fact false   I hold that much less can be known about the universe as a whole than many philosophers are inclined to suppose , I should not therefore assert dogmatically that the universe is other than it is said to be in this or that system, unless the account in question appeared self-contradictory   What I do maintain is that, in view of the mistakes in Bergson's reasoning, his conclusions remain mere imaginative possibilities to be placed alongside of the thousand other possibilities invented by cosmic poets

Mr Carr, however, in spite of an apparent concession in in his first paragraph, proceeds to defend Bergson's arguments , and we must therefore proceed to examine his defence   In supposing Bergson to be a visualizer, it appears I was mistaken, but the important point remains, that his speculation is dominated by the sense of sight to a remarkable extent, and that this seems connected with the importance which he assigns to space.

Mr. Carr next considers the distinction which I emphasize between (1) the general concept Number, (2) the particular numbers, (3) the various collections to which numbers are applicable. He says I allow " that Bergson's doctrine that intellectual apprehension compels us to have recourse to an extended image is true of meaning (3) " This is a misunderstanding ; the view in question is examined and rejected in the paragraph on p 15 beginning " But apart from the question of numbers, shall we admit Bergson's contention that every plurality of separate units involves space ? " Hence the inferences drawn by Mr. Carr from my supposed concession fall to the ground

The next question raised, as to the order in which we come to know the above three meanings, appears to me logically irrelevant, and it is only under protest that I am willing to consider it. He asks · " Can we apprehend the number 12 if we have never had acquaintance with any particular instance of 12 units ? " He supposes that my answer must be in the negative, because I say that the number 12 is " something which all these collections of 12 units have in common," and he supposes that this is a definition of 12. It is not a definition, and does not have the form of a definition. And I certainly hold that we might apprehend the number 12 without having acquaintance with any particular dozen. I have not, so far as I know, ever been acquainted with a collection of 34,361 units, yet I apprehend the number 34,361. But it is impossible to pursue this topic without raising the whole question of our acquaintance with universals.

With regard to Zeno, Mr Carr says that I remove one paradox only to leave him with a greater. I admit that this impression is partly my fault, and that I have not always been sufficiently careful to display my slavish adherence to common sense. But in the main the impression—which Mr Carr shares with many philosophers who have tried to understand the mathematical theory of infinity and continuity—is due to the almost unconscious drawing of fallacious inferences For instance, if I say "no part of Tristram Shandy's biography would remain permanently unwritten," I am supposed to imply that some day the biography will be finished, which is by no means implied, and in the circumstances supposed is plainly false. This applies to Mr. Carr's doubt whether, on my principles, the tortoise cannot overtake Achilles. I say that, if they go on for ever, every place reached by Achilles will ultimately be reached by the tortoise ; and at first sight this *seems* inconsistent with the statement that, after Achilles has passed the tortoise, the distance between them will continually increase. But this apparent inconsistency disappears as soon as the matter is understood.

With regard to the phrase "from nothing to nothing," Mr. Carr says I ignore Bergson's doctrine that " nothing " is a pseudo-idea. This is a misunderstanding I hold just as strongly as Bergson (though for different reasons) that " nothing " is a pseudo-idea ; I used the phrase, as it ordinarily would be used, as an abbreviation for the phrase " not from anything and not to anything.

With regard to the confusion of subject and object with which I charge Bergson, Mr. Carr says that as regards intuition " so far from the identity of subject and object being a confusion, it is of the very essence of the doctrine." It was precisely my contention that it was of the essence of the doctrine ; but I fail to see how this proves that it is not a confusion It seems to me that only one who has never clearly distinguished subject and object can accept Bergson's " intuition." In the case of memory, this seems particularly evident, since it becomes necessary for Bergson to identify remembering with what is remembered, and therefore to say that whatever is remembered still endures. To say that such identification is of the essence of his doctrine is no defence ; the only valid defence would be to show that remembering is in fact identical with what is remembered.

In conclusion, I must admit that there is an element of question-begging in all refutations of Bergson. When we have shown that this or that doctrine is self-contradictory, we have only shown that it does not appeal to the intellect ; if the intellect is in fact misleading, as Bergson contends, it is useless to employ it against him. It is true that Bergson continually employs it in his own defence, by advancing arguments which plainly are intended to be intellectually satisfying. But this perhaps is a concession to the unconverted : when his philosophy has triumphed, it is to be supposed that argument will cease, and intellect will be lulled to sleep on the heaving sea of intuition. But until that consummation the protests of intellect will continue.

EXPRESS PRINTING WORKS, 36, KING STREET, CAMBRIDGE.

The following addresses delivered before the Society have also been published in pamphlet form and may be obtained from any Cambridge bookseller, or from the Secretary —

Dare to be Wise, by Dr. J. E. McTaggart.

Heresy and Humanity, by Miss J E. Harrison.

The Future of Religion, by G. Bernard Shaw

A Reply to Mr. Shaw, by G K Chesterton

Religion in the University, by F. M. Cornford.

Modern Morality and Modern Toleration, by E. S. P Haynes.

Unanimism, by Miss J. E Harrison

De Haeretico Comburendo, by G. M Trevelyan.

The Historicity of Jesus, being a debate on the Christ-Myth Controversy between J M. Robertson, M.P , and H. G. Wood, M.A.

————

In addition, the following papers read before the Society have been printed in periodicals :—

The Primitive Conception of Death, by Dr. W. H. R Rivers. (*Hibbert Journal,* 1912).

The Problem of an Effective Lay Moral Education, by Harrold Johnson (*International Journal of Ethics,* 1912)

The Creation of Taste, by Holbrook Jackson (*English Review,* 1913).

————

Some particulars of the Society will be found on the following page.

HONORARY MEMBERS.

Prof. E. G Browne.
E Bullough
Prof J B Bury.
G G Chisholm.
F M Cornford.
Sir Francis Darwin.
E J Dent
G Lowes Dickinson.
Prof Arthur Drews
Prof Patrick Geddes
Prof H A Giles
L H G Greenwood
Dr A C Haddon
Prof E W Hobson.
G H Hardy
Miss J. E Harrison.
Professor L T Hobhouse
W E Johnson
J M Keynes
W R M Lamb
Dr J E. McTaggart
Dr. W. McDougall
Prof. H. O Meredith.

G. E. Moore.
V. H. Mottram.
Dr F Muller-Lyer.
Dr C S Myers
Prof R C Punnett.
Dr W H Rivers.
D S Robertson.
Dr G F Rogers
The Hon Bertrand Russell.
Miss E. Sargant
Prof A. C Seward
G Bernard Shaw
J T Sheppard
Miss F. M Stawell.
Prof G F Stout
F J M Stratton
H. W V Temperley.
G M Trevelyan.
Prof W. F Trotter.
Dr. Ivor Tuckett.
V S Vernon Jones
E Vulliamy.
H J. Wolstenholme

COMMITTEE.

President ·
C K. Ogden (Magdalene College).

Treasurer :
W L Scott (Clare College).

Secretary
P Sargant Florence
(Caius College).

A. S. Florence (Newnham
College).

C. Thorne (Clare College).

H. B. Usher (Trinity Hall).

A. L Gardiner (Caius College).

EXTRACT FROM THE LAWS.

2   That the object of the Society be to promote discussion on problems of Religion, Philosophy, and Art.

4.   Membership of the Society shall imply the rejection of all appeal to Authority in the discussion of religious questions.

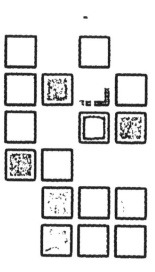

Lightning Source UK Ltd.
Milton Keynes UK
UKOW05f1311020317
295717UK00007B/300/P